To See the Cage is to Leave It
25 Techniques the Few Use to Control the Many

Etienne de la Boetie²

EXECUTIVE DIRECTOR

THE ART OF LIBERTY FOUNDATION

Fair Use Act Disclaimer
FAIR USE

Pro-Tip For Sharing This Book with Others:

This book is best read and gifted as a hard copy. If you want someone to spend time with a written work, then paper is the most inviting, impossible to delete, easier on the eyes, and convenient. Select Portrait, Print on Both Sides of the Paper, and Flip on the Long Side for a dual-sided printer. A double-sided printer will require 41 pages, and a single-sided printer will need 82 pages of paper. Please let this notice memorialize our permission to reprint this book at copy shops and office supply stores, where you can have it spiral or perfect bound.

ISBNs
Hardback, 979-8-89692-576-7 Paperback, 979-8-89692-573-6 Ebook, 979-8-89692-572-9
Available: SeeTheCage.com, Government-Scam.com/Store, Amazon, Draft to Digital

WARNING!! PREPARING THE READER!!

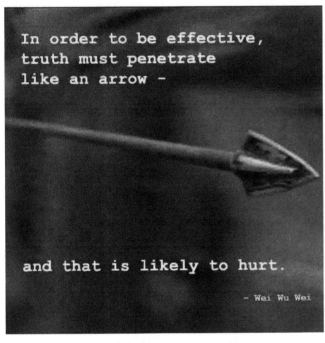

"It is hard to get a man to understand something
when his salary depends
on his not understanding it"
- Upton Sinclair

For many, especially those who work for the "government" or police or serve/served in the military, what you are going to learn in this book is going to be painful.

If you read with an open mind and you can take a step back and analyze what you were told as a child about the legitimacy, desirability, necessity and morality of "Government," you are going to discover that you were tricked... By mandatory schools, scouting and a multi-trillion dollar control-of-perception program of monopoly media and algorithmic censorship on the DARPA Internet... *Just like this author was for decades...* into supporting a system based on lies, propaganda, indoctrination, extortion and violence. The reward comes in knowing the truth because the truth shall, quite literally, set you free.

**To admit that one was wrong is to declare that
you are wiser now than you were before.**

"There are three classes of people: those who see, those who see when they are shown, those who do not see" - Leonardo Da Vinci.

Table of Contents

Table of Contents Continued

Introduction

Would it surprise you to learn that "Government" was never designed to protect life, liberty, and property? Instead, it functions primarily as a sophisticated system for robbing and controlling populations?

The intergenerational organized crime system behind the US "government" (and other governments) is running what can best be characterized as a form of "Pimp Game" on their populations to trick them into an illogical and immoral pseudo-religious belief system. This completely indoctrinated belief system creates two classes of people: "order followers" in the police and military, who agree to set their morality aside and use violence on peaceful people to enforce the "commandments" of the religion or raise revenue on their neighbors. The second class is ordinary citizens who become, in essence, tax-slaves who semi-voluntarily "tithe".

 What makes this system particularly troubling is its use of *proven* psychological manipulation techniques—***the same methods used by disingenuous religions or cults to indoctrinate their followers***. Once you understand these techniques, you'll recognize an unmistakable pattern: The combined forces of banks, the organized crime "government," monopoly mainstream media, and hierarchically controlled puppets in monopoly academic institutions are trying to trick, sucker and "chump" the population toward accepting a system that is against their interests.

 I know this firsthand. Like many Americans, I followed a traditional path—Cub Scouts and Boy Scouts—and even considered a military career. I visited a recruiter with a friend, and we both took the Armed Services Vocational Aptitude Battery (ASVAB) test. The system had me *"Hook, Line and Sinker"* until someone helped me understand the bigger picture. Once I saw how the game was being rigged, everything changed.

 This book will show you exactly how these control mechanisms work. It builds on my previous book *"Government"—The Biggest Scam in History... Exposed!*, which laid the groundwork for understanding this system. My upcoming book *Voluntaryism— How the Only "ISM" Fair for Everyone Leads to Harmony, Prosperity and Good Karma for All* will present the solution: ***REAL*** Freedom!

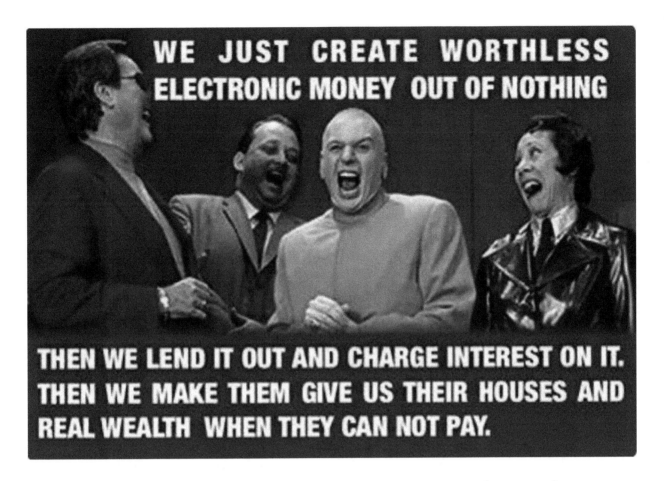

Understanding the Situation: Behind the "US Government" and many other "governments" lies <u>an inter-generational organized crime system centered around banking and central banking</u>. These crooked bankers lobbied and bribed "governments" to "legalize" a technique called <u>fractional reserve banking</u> to create digital dollars and little paper tickets out of thin air, even though it is inflationary and steals the value out of everyone else's money.

This inter-generational organized crime system has bought up the world with the digital dollars and paper tickets they create out of thin air, starting with the monopolized media that puts deception, distraction, and cultural debasement on every screen to hide/obfuscate their criminal activities.

Asset managers, including <u>Blackrock, Vanguard, and State Street,</u> appear to manage the ownership of the companies stolen through fractional reserve banking. At the same time, the C-level executives are apparently organized and coordinated into front organizations that include the <u>World Economic Forum,</u> the <u>Council on Foreign Relations, the Trilateral Commission, and the Bilderberg Group.</u>

Who Is Stealing the Value Out of Our Money?

How the Organized Crime Banks Use "Government" to Rob You to Pay for A Monopoly Media "Propaganda Matrix" of Lies and Deception

Imagine I have dollar and you have a dollar and we have the only two dollars in the world

I own **50%** of the world's wealth and you own **50%** of the world's wealth.

After Organized Crime Central Banking / Fractional Reserve Banking

Now a bank, central bank or "government" comes along and creates two more dollars using fractional reserve banking, "quantitative easing" and/or a printing press/digital dollar creation.

Now you and I have been reduced to owning **25%** of the world's wealth, and the bank or "government" has stolen **50%** of the world's wealth...

Bank/Central Bank Creates two additional Dollars
They have now stolen **50%** of the World's Wealth

Now imagine if they took the astronomical "profits" from stealing the value out of everyone's money and bought up the media, search engines, social media and funded only crooked politicians to ensure that (almost) everything you ever saw on a screen was deception, distraction, and/or cultural debasement.
There is a resistance! and its definitely *NOT* Donald Trump and Elon Musk!

ArtOfLiberty.org/inflation   Government-Scam.com   Voluntaryism-Book.org

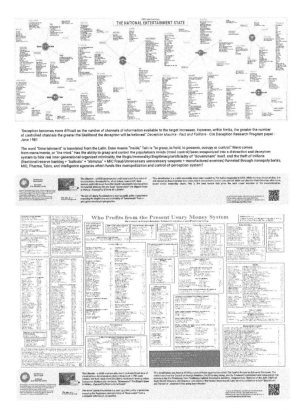

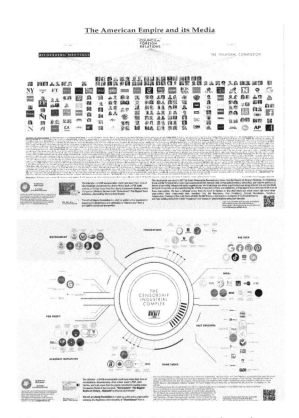

Visualizations from our free poster series: _The White Rose MUCHO GRANDE_ showing the monopolization of everything. The first poster shows the monopolization of the traditional media (television networks, cable, newspapers, radio stations, etc.) into a small handful of six companies operating as a cartel while running hundreds of subsidiaries under different names to offer the illusion of choice and diversity.

The second visualization illustrates how the publishers, editors, and key reporters at dozens of ostensibly unaffiliated media companies are members of three front organizations: the Council on Foreign Relations, the Trilateral Commission, and the Bilderberg Group, where they meet regularly in secure facilities. Interestingly, suspected Mossad blackmail operator Jeffrey Epstein was a member of all three of these organizations.

The third visualization shows that those same three organizations have also installed their members in **_every major power center in the US "government" for decades, through both Republican and Democratic administrations._**

The final visualization is from Matt Taibi's Racket News. It shows a network of 3-4 dozen search engines, social media companies, NGOs, government agencies, and "fact checkers" found to be censoring information algorithmically on the DARPA Internet during "The Covid," including factual information on vaccine dangers.

Other visualizations in the series show the monopolization of **_everything_**, including seed companies, consumer goods, beverages, airlines, defense contractors, and breweries. Check out all the full high-res versions ArtOfLiberty.org/White-Rose

11

TThroughout history, a sophisticated network of power brokers has operated in the shadows, manipulating governmental structures to their advantage. This shadowy consortium has maintained its grip on authority not through force alone, but through carefully crafted systems of influence passed down through generations.

Their methods of securing public compliance and loyalty bear striking similarities to the psychological techniques employed by cult leaders. By weaving their influence into the very fabric of society, they've created an almost religious devotion to their constructed systems of power, all while systematically extracting resources from the very population they claim to serve.

Their secret pseudo-religion is called **Statism**— the indoctrinated belief in having a "government" in the first place, allegiance to it, and the poisonous, indoctrinated worldview that legitimizes the willingness to use violence against peaceful people through the police and military.

Statism is the completely *indoctrinated* belief in the desirability, necessity, and legitimacy of having a *State* ("Government"), *even though there is no ironclad law of the universe that "government" is needed, desirable, necessary, or legitimate.* Everyone would be wealthier, and the world would be more harmonious without "government," but these ideas are never presented in mandatory schools or in the monopoly media.

The idea of having a "government" is a wholly indoctrinated belief system — it has been mandatorily taught to the overwhelming majority of the public through government schools and private schools where the "government" controls instructional content through accreditation, textbook consolidation, and tradition.

"IS NOT THE STATE AN IDOL? IS IT NOT LIKE ANY GRAVEN IMAGE INTO WHICH MEN HAVE READ SUPERNATURAL POWERS AND SUPERHUMAN CAPACITIES? THE STATE CAN FEED US WHEN WE ARE HUNGRY, HEAL US WHEN WE ARE ILL: IT CAN RAISE WAGES AND LOWER PRICES, EVEN AT THE SAME TIME: IT CAN EDUCATE OUR CHILDREN WITHOUT COST: IT CAN PROVIDE US AGAINST THE CONTINGENCIES OF OLD AGE: WHAT CANNOT THE STATE DO FOR US IF ONLY WE HAVE FAITH IN IT?"
- Frank Chodorov

ArtofLiberty.org   Government-Scam.com

The Libertarian Christian Institute breaks down the case, chapter and verse, for the idolatry of Statism in their free eBook: The Idolatry of Statism - Why Christians Should Oppose Nationalism, which we syndicate in our uncensorable flash drive of freedom: The Liberator

Statism is a pseudo-religious belief because "Government" is not a physical entity that can be touched. Instead, it's presented as a supernatural entity that promises to make the world a better place for true believers who have accepted the belief system into their worldview. The multigenerational organized crime system ruling the planet from behind the scenes uses the same techniques that disingenuous religions and manipulative cults use on their followers to brainwash the masses into accepting a ruling class.

KAREN TOLD ME

IT WASN'T A CULT

One of the ugliest, stone-cold truths about the United States is that the organized crime system behind "government" has been and continues to use classic, textbook, unethically manipulative cult-indoctrination techniques on the population to get them to accept a ruling class and tax slavery. From mandatory schools and scouting programs indoctrinating the pseudo-religion of <u>Statism</u> in kids to <u>a monopoly media system making the "government" the hero in movies and tell-a-vision shows</u> to "product placing" the American flag into moments of high positive emotion in blockbuster movies, the population is being tricked into identifying as an "American" *(versus a free and independent human being)* and paying "taxes" (tithes) to a ruling class.

The results range from the religiously faithful humorously wearing the flag of the system that is robbing, tax-farming, and controlling them, to the incredible sadness of some shaving their heads, wearing the uni-form (single form) of artificially engineered conformity and agreeing to murder whomever they are told by the "church leadership."

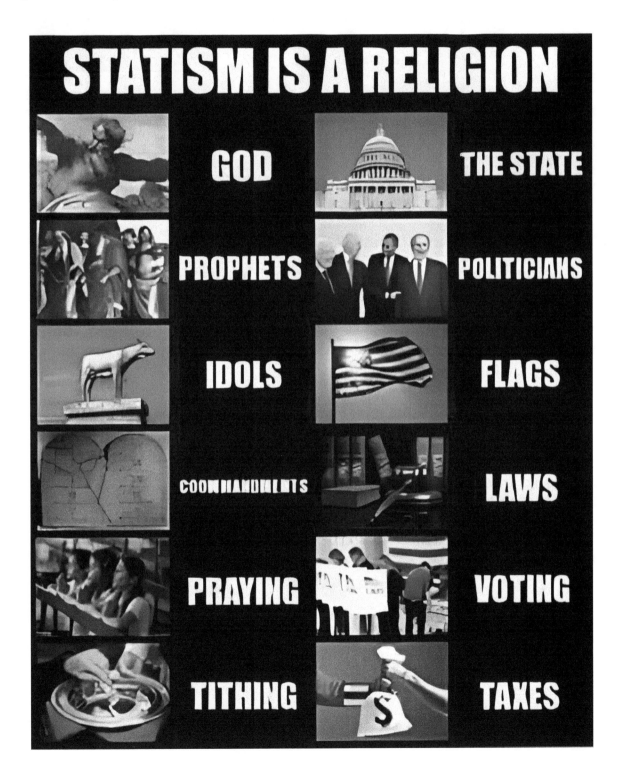

What is being hidden behind "age restriction" in this video on <u>The Most Dangerous Religion?</u> <u>Click HERE for a non-age restricted version on Odysee.</u>

Are you really an "American" just because you were born into a geographical area controlled by an intergenerational organized crime system running "government" on you?

Do you have to be a "Crip" if you are born in South Central Los Angeles?

Do you have to be a "Blood" if you live in Compton, California?

OR, are you ***<u>a free and independent human being</u>*** trapped in a system that is robbing and tax-farming the population using ***trickery*** and shave-headed cult members willing to use violence on peaceful people to enforce the commandments of an artificially indoctrinated statist religion on their friends, family, and neighbors?

But...What Would We Do Without "Government"?
What is the Alternative?
REAL Freedom... Voluntaryism!

The alternative —deliberately hidden by mandatory "government" schools and monopoly media —is _**REAL**_ Freedom: _Voluntaryism_. We don't really need "government". Everything it does (besides redistribution, which is immoral) would be done better, faster, and cheaper by the free market, mutual aid societies, non-profits, insurance companies, armed protective service providers, arbitration companies, co-ops and genuine charities.

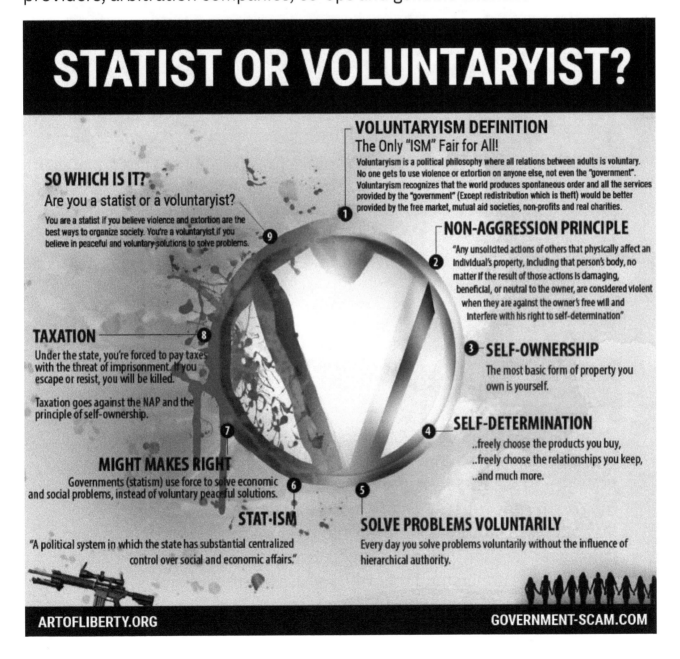

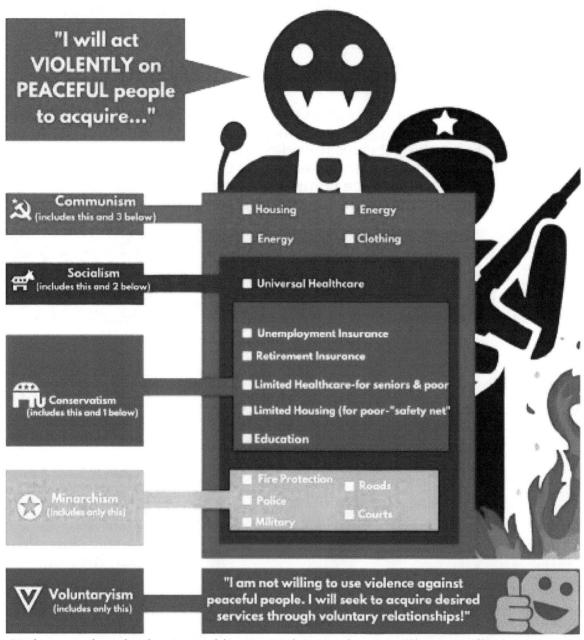

Voluntaryism is the "good karma" alternative you'll never find discussed in mainstream media (*or Mainstream Alternative Media!*), nor will you see it *"Suggested For You"* by Facebook or *"Recommended for You"* by YouTube. It's more moral and logical than Statism. While Statists try to impose their preferred ruler on friends, neighbors, and colleagues through violence to achieve socio-political goals, voluntaryists understand that the world is a self-organizing system. The free market, mutual aid societies, non-profits, insurance companies, co-ops, and genuine charities would provide all legitimate non-redistributive services currently monopolized by "government," creating a more harmonious and prosperous society.

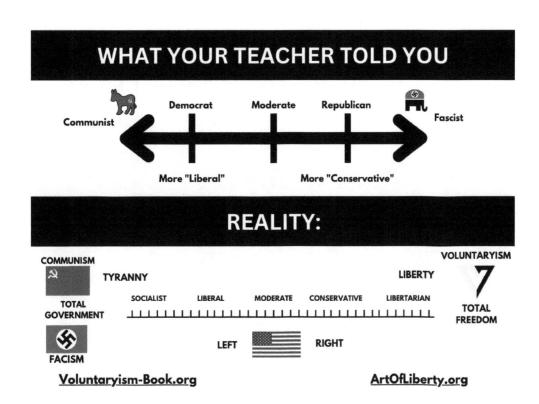

Because it's morally and logically impossible to have a moral, legitimate government, Voluntaryism is the only political philosophy that is fair to everyone. No one gets the "Ring of Power" because there isn't one. No one has special "Rights" that others don't possess, and no one, *especially not the "government,"* has an exemption from morality.

Where do Voluntaryists Fit on the Political Spectrum?

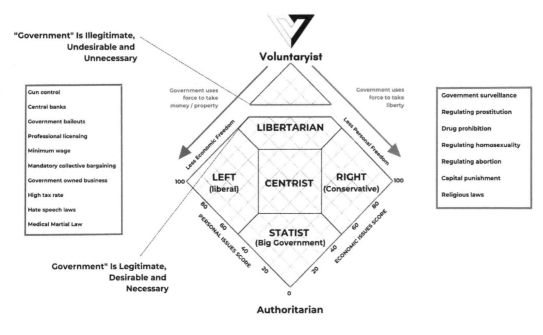

25 Unethical, Cult-Creation Techniques the Government & Media Are Using Against Everyone

1. Controlling the information that kids receive about the legitimacy, desirability and necessity of having a "government" in _mandatory_ schools running the Prussian model of education - Kids are forced to attend "public" schools run by the "government" where they are subject to an educational model openly developed to install allegiance and obedience into the Prussian population so they would fight for a Prussian feudal monarchy. The same techniques are being used on kids today, and Kindergarten is a Prussian word for "Garden to Raise Children." Unsaid is: "In the ideology of the State!"

Children are taught that "government" is legitimate, desirable and necessary before they are old enough to evaluate the logic and morality of the claim for themselves.

Public school is where the catechism is taught.

Indoctrination Techniques include:

- Common Prayer: The pledge of allegiance at school and the national anthem at sporting events
- Civics and social studies that teach kids the Statist worldview
- Focus on learning about the Presidents (Popes) and the legitimacy of "government"
- Socialization of the enforcement class (police) through the D.A.R.E. program
- Promotion of military, selective service, and military recruiters in schools

Obedience Techniques include:

- The inability to leave or even go to the bathroom without permission
- Public shaming (Red, Yellow, Green) and collective punishment
- Responding to Pavlovian bells, walking in line, obedience to police, etc
- Ability to be searched and controlled at any time by "government" employees conditions kids to subserviency

2. Government-affiliated scouting programs indoctrinate kids into the pseudo-religion of Statism with flag worship, allegiance oaths, indoctrinated respect/legitimacy and awards (Cub Scout Adventure Loops and Boy Scout Merit Badges) for learning and regurgitating the doctrine of the religion. Kids are groomed for military and police service through indoctrination into the Uni-Form (The Single Form), which is an artificially engineered group conformity with social pressure placed on kids to participate. When they reach the Boy Scout Explorer program, they will be segmented away from the population to police stations and military bases where they will be further conditioned with some militarized, their heads shaved to create a further artificial group conformity, given guns and taught how to kill for the State. Many will be sexually abused. A 2011 L.A. Weekly investigation revealed that the Law Enforcement Explorer program alone had over 100 incidents of participating police officers engaging in sex with participants, with the overwhelming majority being underage. These were just the cases where the officers were caught.

Hitler Describes the Cub Scouts, Boy Scouts, Explorers, Young Marines, JROTC, Americorp, and the US Military

"These boys and girls enter our organizations [at] ten years of age, and often for the first time get a little fresh air; after four years of the Young Folk, they go on to the Hitler Youth, where we have them for another four years . . . And even if they are still not complete National Socialists [Statists], they go to Labor Service and are smoothed out there for another six, seven months . . . And whatever class consciousness or social status might still be left . . . the Wehrmacht [German armed forces] will take care of that." **—Adolf Hitler** (1938)

Government-Scam.com   **ArtOfLiberty.org**

24

Many don't realize this, but <u>some high schools</u> in the United States are openly run by the military, including the Marines, who, at one time, ran eight high schools in Chicago alone and the <u>Young Marines</u>, a feeder program that ***recruits kids as young as eight years old*** and runs posts and programs for kids around the country.

3.**<u>Junior Reserve Officer Training Corp (JROTC)</u>** - The government's mandatory school system offers trips, monetary incentives, uni-forms, and other rewards to children to begin indoctrinating love of the uni-form and obedience to hierarchical command and control. They are given guns and taught how to kill to enforce the commandments of the church leadership.

4. **Police "Training"** - Police are also segmented away from the general population and, delusionally, trained that because they represent "government," they have rights that other people don't have and that it is OK for them to use violence on peaceful people to enforce the "law" (commandments) of the Statist religion and/or rob their neighbors to raise revenue. Their heads are shaved, and they are made to wear the uni-form (single form) of an artificially engineered conformity. They wear patches and badges to signify they are part of a special group. They will be forced to arrest people for victimless crimes, which aren't really crimes at all and make the participating police officers the actual criminals, which further compacts them into an unhealthy group dynamic vs. the rest of the population. They will be paid over and above what most could earn for comparably skilled labor, trapping many financially with the carrot of gold-plated pensions to keep them on the job, living off money stolen from others at the point of a gun.

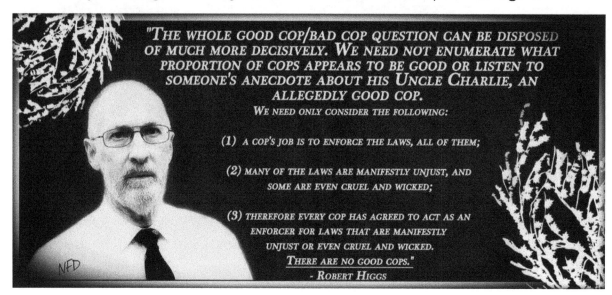

"THE WHOLE GOOD COP/BAD COP QUESTION CAN BE DISPOSED OF MUCH MORE DECISIVELY. WE NEED NOT ENUMERATE WHAT PROPORTION OF COPS APPEARS TO BE GOOD OR LISTEN TO SOMEONE'S ANECDOTE ABOUT HIS UNCLE CHARLIE, AN ALLEGEDLY GOOD COP.
WE NEED ONLY CONSIDER THE FOLLOWING:

(1) A COP'S JOB IS TO ENFORCE THE LAWS, ALL OF THEM;

(2) MANY OF THE LAWS ARE MANIFESTLY UNJUST, AND SOME ARE EVEN CRUEL AND WICKED;

(3) THEREFORE EVERY COP HAS AGREED TO ACT AS AN ENFORCER FOR LAWS THAT ARE MANIFESTLY UNJUST OR EVEN CRUEL AND WICKED. THERE ARE NO GOOD COPS."
- ROBERT HIGGS

5. Military "Basic Training" - The military is segmented away from the general population and is isolated onto military bases where their communications with the outside world are curtailed. During "basic training," they are forced to undergo a variety of unethically manipulative techniques, including verbal and physical abuse, excessive stress, degradation and humiliation, sleep deprivation, isolation and the artificial conformity of the uni-form (single form) and shaved heads replacing individual physical appearance with a group appearance further reinforcing the artificially created group dynamic. The services are notorious for inciting peer pressure and collective punishment, including "blanket parties" where the non-conforming are beaten with improvised flails (soap bars or locks wrapped in a towel/sock).

The Marines take the doors off the stalls in the bathroom so recruits can't have even a moment of privacy to reflect on what is being done to them or the fact that they are committing to murder whomever the church leadership tells them to. They are injected with debilitating "vaccines" and forced to sing march cadences that normalize murder.

 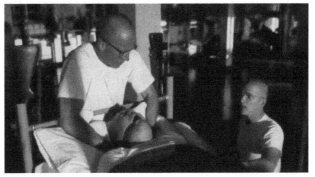

Toilets at USMC Boot Camp don't offer a moment of privacy for self-reflection (left), while the non-conforming are subject to the brutality of the "blanket party" as revenge for the collective punishment depicted in Full Metal Jacket (right)

27

I can't wait for my sons to die for freedom!

Statism is the only modern religion that still requires human sacrifice

Both the military as a whole and USMC Drill Sergeants in particular, have suicide rates well over the national average.

Left, right, left, right, left, right, kill!
Left, right, left, right, you know I will!
Went to the playground, where all the kiddies play,
Pull out my Uzi, and I begin to spray!
Left, right, left, right, left, right, kill!
Left, right, left, right, you know I will!
Go to the mall, where all the ladies shop,
Pull out my machete, and I begin to chop!
Left, right, left, right, left, right, kill!
Left, right, left, right, you know I will!

USMC Marching Cadence

6. Information to the Military, Intelligence Agencies, and Federal/State Law Enforcement Being Hierarchically Controlled.

   a. **Techniques include:**

   i. Top Secret Networks Where Communication is Tightly Monitored. - NIPRnet and SIPRnet as examples.
   ii. Armed Forces Television and Armed Forces Radio - Control of what the troops see and listen to reinforce the narrative.
   iii. Controlled News Feeds in Situation Rooms = CNN and Fox and Bloomberg and other cartel media companies reinforce the official story of events like 9-11, the Waco Massacre, the Oklahoma City Bombing, the Boston Marathon Bombing and other false flags and propaganda crimes.
   iv. Department of Homeland Security "Fusion Centers" are Embedded on Top of State Police and Big City Police Departments to control information to those departments and semi-federalize the departments.
   v. Top Secret Classification makes it impossible to question certain orders and narratives being passed down the chain of command and disseminated to the troops or civilians through InfraGuard.

7. The Artificially Indoctrinated Holy Symbol of the American Flag is Manipulatively Woven Into the Burial Ceremony of the Deceased - A trick to get the participants to associate the memory of their beloved deceased with the flag even though it is the policies of the "church leadership" that is frequently responsible for their deaths.

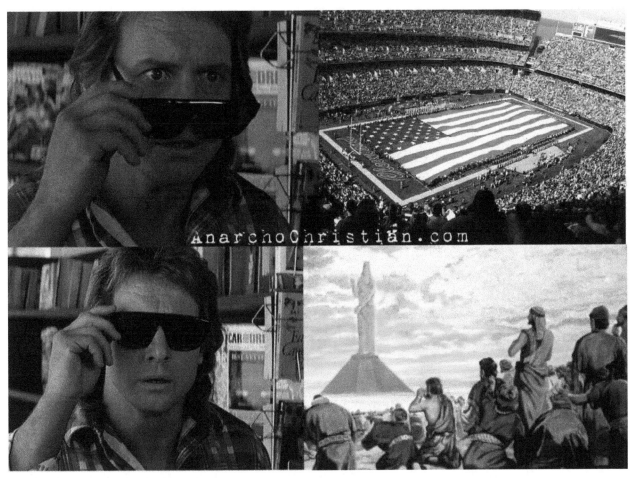

8. Paid-For Flag Worship Woven Into Stadium Events and Sports - Weaving flag worship ceremonies into stadium events is another type of unethically manipulative product placement of the flag and "Anchoring" technique. Everyone loves a football or baseball game, so the organized crime system pays teams, <u>previously as much as $53 million a year</u>, to add flag worship events and military jet flyovers to important games to "anchor" the excitement and good times of an outdoor event to the flag and "government." The fact that the US "government" is paying the teams to participate is proof that it is artificial.

It is, technically, a form of idolatry, as broken down in detail in the free book: _The Idolatry of Statism - Why Christians Should Oppose Nationalism_, from the Libertarian Christian Institute, which we also syndicate in our uncensorable flash drive of freedom: _The Liberator_

Many times the patriotic content is secretly "product-placed" into the games. In the 2025 Super Bowl half-time show, the back up dancers for Kendrick Lamar were dressed in Red, White and Blue and formed an American Flag while performer SZA had American Flags prominently on his jacket.

Unethically Manipulative Techniques Used By Organized Crime's Monopoly Media to Secretly Indoctrinate the Population Into the Religion of Statism

9. The "Government" is Always the Hero - Because the Pentagon and Intelligence Agencies are Paying for it! - Whether it is Tom Cruise saving the world as CIA agent Ethan Hunt or the President of the United States flying fighter jets to save the world from invading aliens in the movie *Independence Day*, the organized crime "government" has been secretly paying Hollywood to weave propaganda and product placement of the American flag into moments of high positive emotion to trick the population into identifying as "Americans." The award-winning documentary ***Theatres of War*** exposes the Pentagon and intelligence agencies controlling the content of ***thousands*** of movies and ***thousands*** of television shows.

The article *Documents Expose how Hollywood Promotes War on Behalf of the Pentagon, CIA and NSA. The US Military Intelligence Agencies have Influenced over 1,800 Movies and TV Shows* by Tom Secker and Matthew Alford, breaks down much of the evidence in the documentary and is included in the Art of Liberty Foundation's Flash Drive of Freedom: *The Liberator*.

The award-winning documentary Theatres of War exposes the Department of Defense and intelligence agency involvement in more than 1,000 movies and 1,000 tell-a-vision shows.
Click Image Above or Scan QR Code to Watch Short 1:51 Trailer.

This television sign-off video from the 1960s has secret words embedded into the scrolling text of the video designed to "Chump" the audience into going along with the "government." Click the image or Scan the QR Code to watch short 4:09 video

10. Subliminal Programming—The "government" and monopoly media have been caught using subliminal programming secretly inserted into tell-a-vision "programming" to propagandize the population. In this example, <u>a 1960 "Television Sign Off Message" played at the end of each broadcast day when people were tired and in a highly suggestible alpha brain wave state was found to contain creepy subliminal messages about "obeying the government."</u>

The messages found in the video above are:

TRUST THE US GOVERNMENT

GOD IS REAL GOD IS WATCHING

BELIEVE IN GOVERNMENT GOD

REBELLION WILL NOT BE TOLERATED

OBEY CONSUME OBEY CONSUME

BUY ULTRA BUY NAOMI

WORSHIP CONSUME OBEY BELIEVE

DO NOT QUESTION GOVERNMENT

11. "Anchoring" the Flag to Moments of High Positive Emotion -

Anchoring is a common advertising technique where a product is "anchored" to a song or cute character in a commercial. Frequently, movies will work the audience up to a moment of high positive emotion and then show them the flag at the apex of the emotional journey the movie is traveling. Matt Damon escaping from Mars in the movie *The Martian,* where the entire film builds to his escape from Mars and then immediately cuts to Earth, where people are waving American flags and Mission Control, where there are giant American flags on the wall, secretly cementing the exhilaration of his escape to the flag.

Other examples include Rocky's win for the USA, in which he wears a US flag to Top Gun Maverick, Superman flying around the world carrying a giant American flag on a flagpole, and Captain America.

*This short video features 469 product placements of
the American flag in just 12 Michael Bay movies.
Click the Image Above or Scan QR Code to Watch the Short 8:32 Video.*

**12. Secretly "Product Placing" the Flag Dozens of Times Across
Thousands of Movies and Television Shows -** We covered the technique
of ***Anchoring*** where the flag is "anchored" to scenes of high positive
emotion. However, another method saturates the flag dozens of times in
a single movie or shows the flag in a context written to make the flag
appealing or reinforce artificial history or tap emotional heartstrings or a
dozen other ways to strengthen an artificially indoctrinated herd
mentality on the population secretly.

13. American Flag is Woven Into Sexually Appealing Advertising - A different form of product placement of the American flag is simply paying cartel companies and publications to include photos of sexually attractive women wearing the flag frequently with subliminal suggestions like: ***"God, This is a Great Country!"***

14. Trick Photography and Religious Iconography - The monopoly media secretly propagandizing the population into an artificial worldview will frequently:

- o Photograph leaders in front of religious symbolism
- o Use trick photography or photoshop to openly or secretly add religious iconography to pictures of the President
- o Add religious symbolism to pictures of the "Pope" of the indoctrinated religion
- o Include religious symbols for other "church leaders" in the senate or executive branch

The goal is to subconsciously trick the population into identifying the artificially indoctrinated leaders as "holy."

15. Adding the Flag to NBA backboards and NFL football helmets so fans subconsciously associate the flag with the exhilaration of the goal
—NFL players are forbidden to remove the flags from their helmets.

16. Exploiting Behavioral Psychology to Satisfy (Most) People's Biological Desire for a Leader / Father Figure - <u>Evolutionary leadership theory</u> posits that most humans have an innate, biological desire for a leader as an evolutionary survival mechanism from our tribal past. Inter-generational organized crime leverages their understanding of behavioral psychology to offer the choice of two different potential puppet leaders to become "Pope" of the indoctrinated religion: A "Blue" Government Leader marketed to appeal to urban liberals and the "Red" Government Leader designed to appeal to rural conservatives. Many people fall for the fake <u>"Hobson's Choice"</u> and begin to self-identify with their preferred "leader."

It is easy to manipulate a pre-determined outcome by having one leader presented by the monopoly media as worse than the other to trick the population into *"voting for ~~the lesser~~ evil."*

Meet the new boss...

TWEEDLE DEE

- "THE COVID"
- FORCING UNNECESSARY VACCINES
- TAXING/THEFTING YOU
- THEM GIVING ORDERS, YOU OBEYING
- NSA/CIA SURVEILLANCE
- FASCIST CRONY CAPITALISM
- PRIVATE PRISONS FOR VICTIMLESS CRIMES
- REGULATORY CAPTURE
- NO BID CONTRACTS
- TRILLIONS MISSING FROM THE PENTAGON
- TSA MOLESTATION AND SECURITY THEATRE
- FRACTIONAL RESERVE BANKING
- BANK AND COVID "BAILOUTS"
- AMA MONOPOLY MEDICINE
- MANDATORY "GOVERNMENT" SCHOOLS
- FALSE FLAG BIO-TERRORISM FOR POLICE STATE

www.ArtOfLiberty.org

TWEEDLE DUM

- "THE COVID"
- FORCING UNNECESSARY VACCINES
- TAXING/THEFTING YOU
- THEM GIVING ORDERS, YOU OBEYING
- NSA/CIA SURVEILLANCE
- FASCIST CRONY CAPITALISM
- PRIVATE PRISONS FOR VICTIMLESS CRIMES
- REGULATORY CAPTURE
- NO BID CONTRACTS
- TRILLIONS MISSING FROM THE PENTAGON
- TSA MOLESTATION AND SECURITY THEATRE
- FRACTIONAL RESERVE BANKING
- BANK AND COVID "BAILOUTS"
- AMA MONOPOLY MEDICINE
- MANDATORY "GOVERNMENT" SCHOOLS
- FALSE FLAG BIO-TERRORISM FOR POLICE STATE

www.Government-Scam.com

...Same as the old boss!

The "leaders" might appear different on the surface, **_BUT_** *will be completely in "Lock Step"* on issues important to the owners.

SWEET TREAT: Ice cream shops in 42 states are participating in the 'I Pledge Project,' which promises kids under 12 a free scoop of ice cream if they recite the Pledge of Allegiance by heart. Learn more about this patriotic effort: https://trib.al/NIONb4

Free ice cream scoop promised to kids if they recite Pledge of Allegiance

The man behind the I Pledge Project selling the indoctrinated pseudo-religion of Statism to kids is Hollywood propagandist Stratton Leopold. He is the executive producer behind movies that glorify the organized crime CIA and "government," including *The Sum of All Fears* and *Mission Impossible III*. Search Engine: *The Religion of Statism, 15 Classic "Textbook" Cult-Indoctrination Techniques the Organized Crime "Government" Uses on its Tax Slaves* and/or *The Shady History of the Pledge of Allegiance* by Etienne de la Boetie2

ArtOfLiberty.org   Government-Scam.com   ArtOfLIberty.Substack.com

17. Giving Kids Ice Cream (Sugar... a Drug that Delivers a Sensory Pleasure to the Brain) for Reciting the Pledge of Allegiance—The I Pledge Project, run by Hollywood propagandist Stratton Leopold, gives free ice cream cones (refined sugar... a drug that delivers a sensory pleasure to the brain) to kids under 12 who recite the pledge of allegiance by heart.

Stratton Leopold is a Hollywood propagandist behind movies that glorify the "government" and intelligence agencies, including *The Sum of All Fears* and *Mission Impossible III*. Check out our article, *The Shady History of the Pledge of Allegiance*, for more info on the Freemason propagandists behind the Pledge of Allegiance.

Comedy Troupe "The Whitest Kids U Know" Mocks The Unethically Manipulative Pledge. Wait for it... wait for it... Click or Scan the QR code to Watch this Short 1:24 video...

Heartbreaking: Annoying Kid That Refused to Do Pledge of Allegiance in High School Was 100% Right

Full story: thehardtimes.net

18. Paying the Population to Pledge Their Support to the Shady Con-stitution -

During the 2024 election, <u>Pentagon, intelligence agency and NASA contractor Elon Musk</u>, who has received over $19 billion in government contracts and $5 billion+ in tax credits and carbon offsets for his electric vehicles, began paying registered voters between $47-$100 to sign a petition supporting the 1st and 2nd amendment to the <u>shady Con-stitition</u>, the document that supposedly enables the organized crime "government" to engage in the "taxation (theft)" that ultimately funnels its way to Pentagon contractor Musk. Musk then began giving away $1,000,000 a day to random petition signers, ensuring widespread media coverage of the little scam.

19. Pro-Statist Propaganda Inserted into Facebook, TikTok, Instagram, and other social media sites. - The organized crime "government" and their partners in the monopoly media, including social media, search engines, Twitter/X, Reddit, and other platforms, are putting patriotic content into your feed, including Facebook posts "Suggested For You" and YouTube videos "Recommended for You." which promote a wholly false and indoctrinated world view on the population.

Social Media apps recommend politicians and controlled opposition voices, boosting the visibility of content generated by these voices while suppressing authentic voices. This suppression, demonetization, and shadow banning of authentic voices is known as ***"Freedom of Speech but Not Reach,"*** where you can publish something, but the organized crime monopoly media will suppress it even if others have subscribed to your content.

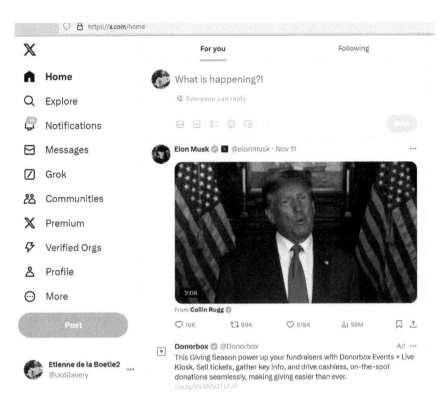

In my article *Are Jake Paul and Elon Musk Artificially Created "High-Status Monkeys" to Steer Perception with Netflix and X?*, I break down the behavioral psychology of how monkeys and humans are biologically pre-disposed to pay attention to "high-status monkeys" (Celebrities) and make the case that Elon Musk, Jake Paul, and Donald Trump are manufactured "high-status monkeys"/Celebrities who has been given social media platforms that leverages this behavior psychology to focus society's attention in an unethically manipulative way.

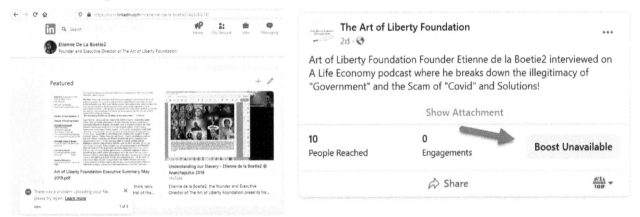

Both Linked In and Facebook Refuse to Let Us "Boost Posts" or Advertise and we are shadow banned on both platforms as well.

At the same time that the organized crime "government" is amplifying their propaganda using Musk and X, authentic voices are being shadow-banned, deindexed, demonetized, debanked, and not allowed to advertise, "boost posts" or reach audiences with the truth. Both Google and Facebook refused to allow the Art of Liberty Foundation to advertise <u>Liberty on the Rocks - Sedona - The Voluntaryism Conference</u> because we were exposing that you don't really need "government" with distinguished academics, economists, authors and journalists as just one single example of a dozen+ such ways our content is being suppressed.

20. Kids are Taken to "Mecca" (Washington, DC) in Middle School, Where they Are Taken to the "Cathedral" of the Capital (That looks like the Vatican... for a Reason) and the "Temples" (monuments) to see the "Deities" (Lincoln, Jefferson) Where Everything is Hushed and Reverent

The Statist "Deity" Lincoln in his temple with his hands resting on Roman Faces from which the word Fascism is derived. More info bottom right.

Lincoln Memorial (temple, left) vs. Nashville's reproduction of the Parthenon (temple, right), a Greek temple of the god Athena

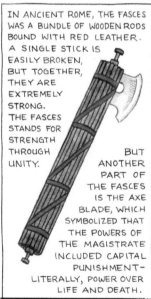

IN ANCIENT ROME, THE FASCES WAS A BUNDLE OF WOODEN RODS BOUND WITH RED LEATHER. A SINGLE STICK IS EASILY BROKEN, BUT TOGETHER, THEY ARE EXTREMELY STRONG. THE FASCES STANDS FOR STRENGTH THROUGH UNITY. BUT ANOTHER PART OF THE FASCES IS THE AXE BLADE, WHICH SYMBOLIZED THAT THE POWERS OF THE MAGISTRATE INCLUDED CAPITAL PUNISHMENT— LITERALLY, POWER OVER LIFE AND DEATH.

The statue of Thomas Jefferson (Left) inside the Jefferson Memorial (temple) in Washington, DC, vs. the statue of the Greek god Athena (middle) inside the Parthenon(temple). On the Right is a Roman Fasces, from which the word "Fascism" is derived. In the picture from his temple in the upper right corner, you can see the deity Abraham Lincoln's hands rest on two Fasces.

21. The Alternative of "No Rulers" is Secretly & Disingenuously Presented to the Public as Chaos and Dystopia by Monopoly "Control of Perception" Media - The word Anarchy doesn't mean "No Rules" It literally means **"No Rulers"** but because the organized crime "Rulers" don't want the public to know there is an option on the menu called "No Rulers" they have used their media and propaganda system to change the meaning of the word: "No Rulers" to mean: *Chaos and Dystopia*.

The weaponized media propaganda system would have you believe that Anarchy (No Rulers) is something to be feared because without "Gubernare Mente"/ Government, there would be Mad Max chaos and murder in the streets.

The reality is that Anarchy is a philosophy of peace. Most anarchists and voluntaryists believe in the Non-Aggression Principle (NAP), where initiating violence is illegitimate except in self-defense or property protection. In a world without rulers, there would still be both a market for justice and armed protective services. Without a monopoly government, the protectors would only focus on actual crime (not victimless crimes or road piracy). They would not delusionally believe they have rights that others don't and could be fired immediately at the first sign of abuse.
Many economists and legal theorists believe anarchy/voluntaryism would lead to dramatically less crime and violence in society, with more prosperity for all.

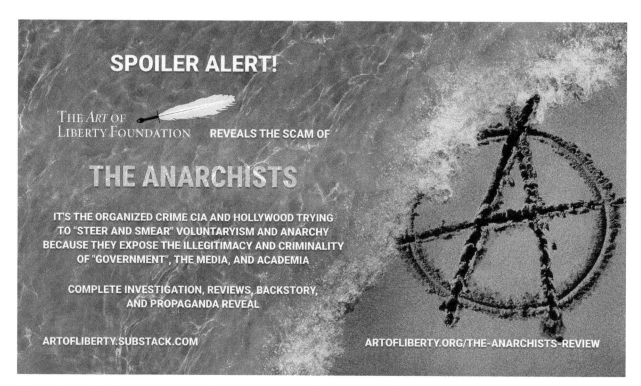

The Art of Liberty Foundation, in our investigation, _Chumped: The Unfortunate Truth About Anarchapulco and HBO's Series: The Anarchists_, breaks down how we believe the intelligence agencies created the Anarchapulco conference to crowd-gather the modern voluntaryist, anarcho-capitalist, and peaceful anarchist movements and steer them into controlled opposition voices/media operations, unintelligible, unwholesome or controlled artists, infighting, etc. while smearing/tarring the movement through association with con men, drug dealers, and murder while stealing the oxygen from legitimate liberty movement conferences, artists and authentic voices.

The operation is very similar to the now-admitted CIA's creation/promotion of admitted CIA asset Gloria Steinem and Ms. Magazine to steer the agency-created and controlled "feminist movement" documented by the book: _The Mighty Wurlitzer - How the CIA Played America_.

Part of the grift was having Time-Warner's HBO (sister company of CNN) produce a "docuseries" called _The Anarchists_ that presented voluntaryists and anarchists as: diseased, nasty, unkempt, adulterous, unstable, drunks with PTSD that flash satanic Baphomets, live in dumps with nasty toilets, where they burn flags, say: _"Fuck the Troops"_, live off their wives, hate Santa Claus, and are associated with the scam of the Bitcoin (alleged to be a Ponzi scheme!) which they get from ATMs they steal from strip clubs... to sum up one of the episodes...

The organized crime "government" is creating fake "documentaries" that **trick** the population into having a negative view of people who don't believe in or support "government."

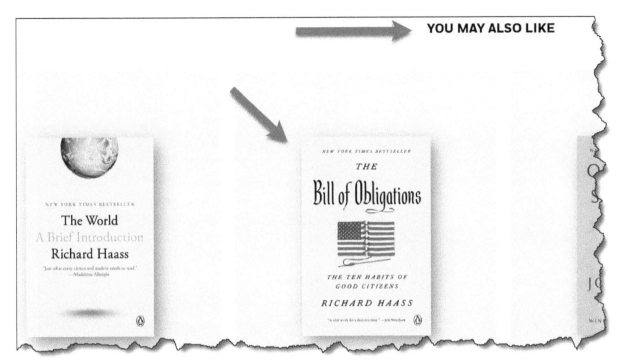

22. Statist Propaganda is given undeserved accolades (New York TImes Bestseller Status, Companion Documentaries, Prominient Reviews, Featured by Cartel media, etc.) and promoted on social media or in cartel bookstores or chain stores like Walmart - I had wrapped up this book at 21 techniques and then while I was finishing the final edits, this book was *"suggested for me"* while checking out another book on the Penguin Random House website. In the example above, Richard Haass, the former President of the Council on Foreign Relations, has published a book where he outlines what he feels are "obligations" to be a "Good Citizen" by virtue of where you were born. In our article *Why the Organized Crime Media Misrepresents Voluntaryism and Peaceful Anarchy as Chaos and Dystopia* on ArtOfLiberty.Substack.com, we break down how another CFR past president, Leslie Gelb, sits on the editorial advisory board for both *Encyclopedia Britannica* and the *Merriam Webster Dictionary* and then show how the definition of anarchy, *__was changed__* from *__"No Rulers"__* TO *__"Chaos and Dystopia"__* by comparing the 1827 definition from the *Webster Dictionary* with the current definition from the *Merriam Webster Dictionary*. When we took a screenshot of the modern definition from the Merriam-Webster website, they were promoting a pro-statist definition of the word: *Socialism*, as a word that people should know and understand, as another example of the technique.

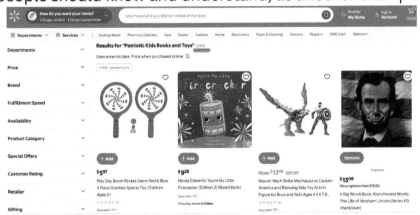

Cartel company Walmart promotes hundreds of statists books, items of clothing, and merchandise, many targeted towards children.

23. The American Flag is Manipulatively Associated with an Emotionally Charged Event, Person, or Group in Propaganda placed in a Highly Visible Area - In this example the names of the victims of the false flag "terrorist" attack of September 11th, 2001 have been superimposed over an American Flag and the resulting propaganda piece, entitled ***"Flag of Honor,"*** has been located in a high traffic area of Miami International Airport, the 10th busiest airport in the United States and 23rd busiest airport in the world.
In the example below, the flags at the US Capitol are frequently flown at "half-mast" to honor someone famous who has died and/or to manipulatively associate the flag with the famous person or specific propaganda point that is then reinforced by the monopoly media.

24. Placing American Flags on Highway Overpasses to Make it Appear the "Government" Has Widespread Support - In 2012 I made an interesting discovery. Before I became a voluntaryist and gave up on what has become obvious rigged elections, I was part of the Ron Paul Revolution. We set up a "sign factory" in a vacant home and pumped out 100+ Ron Paul banners that we would then hang on the highway overpasses leading into Washington, DC. When we were hanging our Ron Paul signs, I noticed that almost all of the American flags on the overpasses leading into Washington, which were numerous, were of the identical size/model and had been attached to the overpasses in the same manner with almost identical clipped zip ties. While I can't prove it, I strongly suspect that these signs were installed by the same crew. Frequently, local governments will hang flags from bridges, light poles, or other high visibility locations using tax payer monies.

25. National holidays and celebrations are associated with the government and flag- In another example of the marketing technique of ***anchoring***, the government has mandated that certain days are set aside to celebrate it. Many Americans overlook the fact that the government is forcing them to work unpaid for five-six months out of the year, and celebrate a single day off that has been, in the case of the 4th of July, linked by the media and pop culture to feasting, drinking, parades, and parties at the lake!

Local governments typically provide fireworks events at taxpayer expense. In the parade examples below, the Boy Scouts are wearing white gloves to handle the holy flag. The artificial honor of the flag could have been technique 26, as the flag can not be thrown away when old but must be "retired" in an official ceremony conducted regularly by American Legion and Veterans of Foreign Wars posts, Cub Scout, Girl Scout and Boy Scout troops, and others. The holy flag is ceremonially burned, and in some cases, its ashes are collected and buried.

Does Belief In and Support for "Government" Meet the Textbook Definition of a Cult?
YES! *Easily*...

What is the Textbook Definition of a Cult?

Cult - \ ˈkəlt \ noun, often attributive - A cult is a group or movement exhibiting a great or **excessive devotion** or dedication to some person, idea, or thing and **employing unethically manipulative techniques of persuasion and control** (e.g., isolation from former friends and family, debilitation, use of special methods to heighten suggestibility and subservience, powerful group pressures, information management, suspension of individuality or critical judgment, promotion of total dependency on the group and fear of leaving it, etc.) **designed to advance the goals of the group's leaders to the actual or possible detriment of members, their families, or the community.**

Confucius famously said, "The beginning of wisdom is to call things by their proper name." Unfortunately, using the word "cult" seems to offend some, but the stone-cold truth is that it is precisely the dynamic at play. If the problem is inter-generational intergenerational organized crime using control of:
- Government schools
- Scouting programs
- Military training
- Police training
- Weaponized media propaganda system

to perpetrate classic, textbook, unethically manipulative "cult indoctrination techniques" on an unsuspecting population, then the solution must be Large Scale Cult Deprogramming, starting with calling the problem by its rightful name.

What is a Cult?
Complete Breakdown with Examples

It takes a lot to get men to murder for a chain of command...

Complete, Word-by-Word Breakdown of the Textbook Definition of a "Cult" on the Previous Page.

Cult - \ ˈkəlt \ noun, often attributive - A cult is a group or movement exhibiting a great or excessive devotion or dedication to some person, idea, or thing

- Nylon cloth (the artificially indoctrinated holy symbol of the "flag"), the "holy documents" of the Constitution [Editor's Note: See our companion article: ***The Shady History of the Con-stitution*** at ArtOfLiberty.Substack.com], the Bill of Rights, the concept of government, "The Law" (I.E. politician scribbles), willingness to murder and use violence on peaceful people when instructed by the hierarchical leadership of the cult.

and employing unethically manipulative techniques of persuasion and control (e.g., collective punishment, isolation from former friends and family)

- Mandatory government schools take kids from families, military bases, commissaries, etc., and segment the shave-headed enforcers from the rest of society to military bases. Both schools, police and military use unethically manipulative indoctrination and obedience techniques described in detail in this book.

- The hidden curriculum of Statism/Obedience in schools, scouting, and police/military training. purposefully crappy education with almost zero (0) focus on logic, morality, the real history of the US, and/or the Trivium (Grammar, Logic, and Rhetoric), IQ lowering Fluoride in water, brain damaging mercury/aluminum in vaccines

use of special methods to heighten suggestibility and subservience

- **Government Schools:** Mandatory gov't "education," can't raise your hand or go to the bathroom without the gov't permission, socialization of enforcement class through D.A.R.E., jROTC, military recruiters in schools, promoted options in career options, etc.

- **Police/Military:** Artificially indoctrinated <u>Statism</u>, Obedience to hierarchical authority even over the individual's own consciousness and basic morality, boot camps, police academies, and "basic training." Brain-damaging adrenaline in the military from "door-kicking" and convoy dangers.

57

powerful group pressures

- Enforced social conformity from an early age I.E., Forced to stand hand over heart for the pledge and national anthem, forced to fight/murder in foreign occupations to protect friends, police "blue wall of silence"/ police perjury/"testilying"

information management

- Hidden propaganda (Product placement of the flag, anchoring, etc.) in 1000+ television programs and 1000+ movies, National Public Radio, Voice of America, Armed Forces Television & Radio, "Ex"CIA agents embedded in the media, the "Echo Chamber" of Fusion Center/ InfraGuard "top secret" intelligence that no one else can verify

- Mandatory gov't schools/tax-supported state universities, police/military "training," secrecy oaths, national security letters,

- Search engine manipulation, state-sponsored "sock-puppet" social media manipulation, "paid for patriotism," and poisoning-the-well of truth news and journalism.

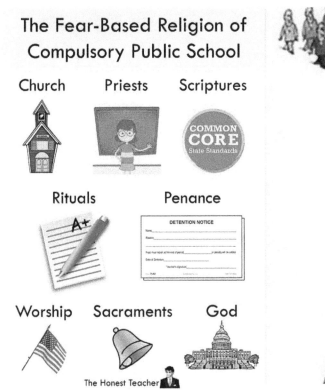

The Fear-Based Religion of Compulsory Public School

Church

Priests

Scriptures
COMMON CORE State Standards

Rituals
A+

Penance
DETENTION NOTICE

Worship

Sacraments
The Honest Teacher

God

PUBLIC SCHOOL

suspension of individuality

- **Gov't Schools:** Everyone's an "American"... *It's been decided for you!*

- **Police / Military: Shaved heads & Uni-Forms similar to other cults**, identical costumes (I.E. uni-forms (the single form, which artificially creates a group identity), badges and patches that signify allegiance to the group, and differentiation from others), willingness to commit violence with/for the group.

Hare Krishnas, Rajneeshpuram members, Heaven's Gate, Jim Jones's People's Temple Members, and Unification Church Members (Moonies) are other organizations that asked adherents to suspend individuality and shave their heads and/or assume the uni-form

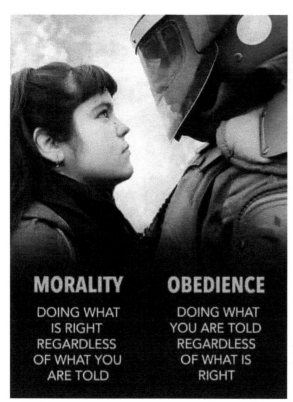

or critical judgment

- Statist obedience to "The Law" (politician scribbles) over their own judgment or basic morality, obedience to hierarchical authority, "order following" *"I don't make the Jim Crow/fugitive slave/plant possession laws.. I just enforce them!"*, "taxpayer" willingness to pay any level of taxation, however damaging to a family's finances.

promotion of total dependency on the group and fear of leaving it, etc.)

- Government employees/police/teachers/military feel trapped by <u>exorbitant salaries</u> and <u>pensions</u> most couldn't get in the private sector (even though everyone would be better off if we rid ourselves of the parasite of organized crime government and their inflationary money and confiscatory taxation)

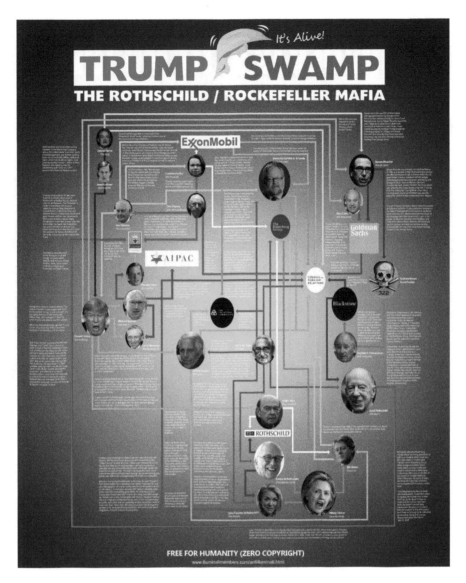

Click on the Image Above to Download a High-Resolution Version from the Dropbox version of our Flash Drive O Freedom: The Liberator

designed to advance the goals of the group's leaders

Trillions of dollars given to private banks and media companies through the "bailouts" and TARP/TALF program recycled into political contributions to the Congressmen who passed it even though 90%+ of the country opposed it, <u>Trillions missing from the Pentagon, hundreds of billions from the post office, Amtrak, HUD and other programs</u>. Monopoly privileges, monopoly patent protections, fractional reserve banking's hidden "inflation tax." Trillions to the Military-Industrial-Complex for unneeded weapons to fight foreign wars based on lies and manufactured intelligence, Mandatory "vaccine" profits to "Big pHARMa". See our companion article: *<u>Who Runs the World? - Organized Crime's Front Groups & Secret Societies</u>* to understand who is at the top of the pyramid.

to the actual or possible detriment of members (karma), their families (karma), or the community.

Population "chumped" and "duped" into believing they "owe" taxes (tithes) to organized crime, the military's willingness to kill foreigners in foreign wars based on obvious lies, police willingness to cage "non-believers" in for-profit prisons and extort money from their neighbors for victimless crimes and road piracy, bureaucrats willingness to participate in the robbing of their friends, neighbors and community for everything from inspections stickers to local, state, and federal "taxes" (theft) while pretending not to understand the morality of the situation.

OK... "Government" is a Scam, and they are trying to run "Game" on me... What do I do now?

Hopefully this book has opened your eyes to the scam of "government" and their partners in crime in the monopoly media. People ask me all the time, **"What can we do to fight this?"** The #1 thing you can do is turn off the tell-a-vision, become educated about what is going on, and then wake up five people to the scam of "government" and get them to commit to waking up five people... and then we win!

Here are some other tips for the average person to fight back, along with my 2nd favorite piece of advice: **Use Cash!** We have to keep cash and barter (Goldbacks, fractional silver, etc.) alive to keep programmable money and the digital control grid of social credit scores off our backs or it is game over.

Become Educated

- Read *"Government" - The Biggest Scam in History... Exposed!* buying a hard copy at <u>Government-Scam.com/Store</u> helps fund the evolution, but there is a free PDF copy available at <u>ArtOfLiberty.org/White-Rose</u> if you can't afford to buy a copy.
- Binge-watch the documentaries and binge-read the important books and articles that we make available for free in the Dropbox version of our uncensorable, credit card-sized flash drive freedom: The Liberator at <u>Government-Scam.com/Liberator</u>
- Turn off the MainStreamMedia, cancel subscriptions to propagandists like Netflix, Amazon Prime Video, and others who have been lying to you and tricking you. We offer a Daily News Summary at <u>https://DailyNewsFromAoLF.substack.com/</u> and a weekly summary of the best of the alternative media at <u>https://FiveMemeFriday.substack.com/</u>

Stop Organized Crime "Governments" and Cartel Banks, Monopoly Media, and Corporations with Global Non Compliance

FIGHT WITH YOUR WALLET TO HURT THEM WHERE IT COUNTS

THIS IS THE ONLY VOICE THEY HEAR LOUD & CLEAR!

1. DO NOT BORROW MONEY FROM MEGA BANKS & STOP USING CREDIT/DEBIT CARDS, USE CASH!!
Cash saves mom & pop businesses 1.5-2.5% AND starves the banks of 1.5-2.5%
Cash starves the organized crime "gov't" by allowing bizs to under-report
Cash is more likely to circulate in the community
The more cash that is used, the harder it is for them to push CBDC or digital $s

2. LEARN TO BARTER FOR GOODS.
try not to use their money, barter when you can, use Goldbacks & silver

3. SHOP LOCAL OWNED STORES & FARMERS MARKETS!
keep your money circulating in your own home-town
Know your farmer, strengthen local food networis, demand organic

4. AVOID LARGE CORPORATE CHAIN STORES SUCH AS COSTCO AMAZON (A Mason?), WAL-MART, OR OTHER CARTEL STORES.
Mega-stores are being financed with unlimited fractional reserve capital and
stocked with Chinese slave labor-made goods as economic warfare against us

5. GROW AS MUCH FOOD HOME AS YOU CAN.
Growing your own food is like printing your own money
Share Your Garden / Co-Garden with Friends & Neighbors

6. BUY USED ITEMS INSTEAD OF NEW.
use local swap n shop, read classifieds/Craig's List, eBay, consignment

7. START A BUSINESS PRODUCING REAL PHYSICAL GOODS AND SELL LOCALLY.
be a productive member of society, start part-time and grow

8. AVOID FAST FOOD CHAIN RESTAURANTS
fast food is laced with toxins/GMOs & Break the Chains!!!

9. SPREAD THE WORD
Distribute *"Government" - The Biggest Scam in History!*
- Get PDF free when you download: *The Liberator*
- Government-Scam.com/Liberator
- Make copies for your friends by buying low-cost flash drives on eBay & copying Liberator drives

Government-Scam.com   **ArtOfLiberty.org**

What Can Government Employees (Local, State, & Federal) Do to Stop The "Deep State" (Organized Crime "Government")

I firmly believe there are many good people in local, state, and even federal governments who have gotten into government service with the best intentions. With the federal "government" and many State governments now openly tyrannical and anti-freedom, what can the good people trapped in a bad system do to limit the harm they are causing in the world?

Here are some of my top tips for good people who got tricked into working for the organized crime "government" and what they can do to mitigate the harm the "government" is causing their friends, neighbors, community, and world.

Understand the Reality of Your Situation: You Are Working for Organized Crime, The "Government" is Illegitimate, and Is Robbing Your Friends, Family and Neighbors. - *My sincerest apologies for having to be the ones to explain this,* but you have been tricked into supporting a system set up by intergenerational organized crime to rob you, your family, friends, and neighbors. "Government" isn't something that was set up to help or protect society. "Government" is a technique... a system used for thousands of years to rob and control society. The root words from Latin are: **Gubernare** = "To Control" & **Mente** = "The Mind" = **Mind Control**

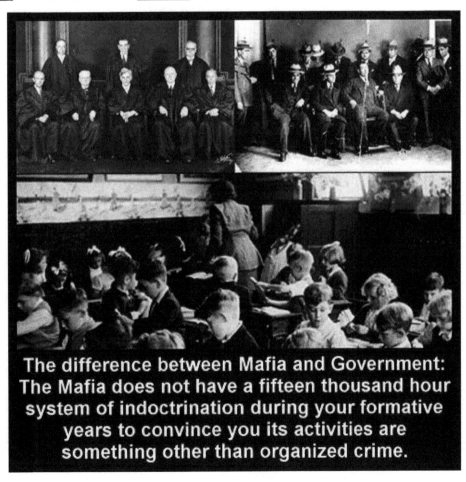

The difference between Mafia and Government: The Mafia does not have a fifteen thousand hour system of indoctrination during your formative years to convince you its activities are something other than organized crime.

When the scam of monarchy / "divine right of kings" was exposed, organized crime developed "democracy" to trick the people into thinking they were in charge but easily controlling the outcome of elections through control of the media, disparity of campaign funds, blackmail, bribery, assassination, and other means.

Democracy itself is an illegitimate concept because nothing, not even if the majority believe it to be so, can make something inherently immoral (theft, extortion, caging non-violent individuals for victimless crimes, etc.) "moral" just because the majority of people decide to vote for something in a political ritual.

Just because the mob wants to lynch black folks or rob Peter to pay Paul doesn't make those obvious crimes moral because the perpetrators outnumber their victims.

The "Gubernare Mente" program raised you to believe that it is OK for you to use violence, extortion and taxation (theft) on overwhelmingly peaceful people because some people are tricked into voting for "government."

You have been conned, duped and "chumped" into participating in an obviously immoral system and robbing your friends and neighbors.

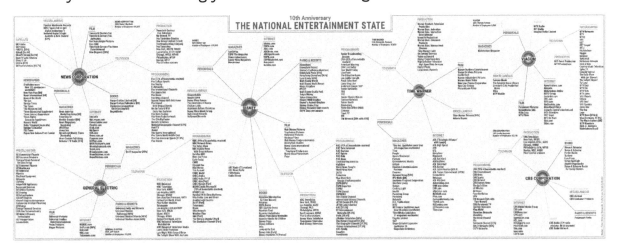

"Deception becomes more difficult as the number of channels of information available to the target increases. However, within limits, the greater the number of controlled channels the greater the likelihood the deception will be believed." *Deception Maxims - Fact and Folklore* - CIA Deception Research Program paper - June 1981

The word "Entertainment" is translated from the Latin: Enter means "inside," Tain is "to grasp, to hold, to possess, occupy or control." Ment comes from mens/mente, or "the mind." Has the ability to grasp and control the population's minds (mind control) been weaponized into a distraction and deception system to hide real inter-generational organized criminality, the illogic/immorality/illegitimacy/artificiality of "Government" itself, and the theft of trillions (fractional reserve banking + "bailouts" + "stimulus" + MIC Fraud/Unnecessary unnecessary weapons + manufactured enemies) funneled through monopoly banks, MIC, Pharma, Telco, and intelligence agencies which funds this monopolization and control-of-perception system?

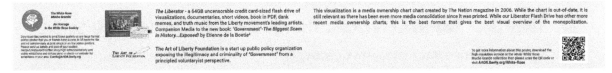

__An Art of Liberty Foundation White Rose MUCHO GRANDE poster showing six monopoly media companies running hundreds of subsidiaries but operating as a cartel to control the information that the population receives about the legitimacy, necessity and desirability of having a "government".__
__This poster and others are available at ArtOfLiberty.org/White-Rose__

Understand the Organized Crime System is Controlling the Information You Have Been Receiving Through Mandatory Schools, Scouting, Monopolized Media and Algorithmic Censorship of the DARPA Internet - The banksters running the organized crime "government" have used fractional reserve banking to buy up and monopolize the media into a small handful of companies running hundreds of subsidiaries to control the information you have been receiving about the legitimacy of "government."

JUDGES, COPS, AND GOVERNMENT EMPLOYEES DON'T PAY TAXES

"TAXES" IS THE MONEY STOLEN BY "GOVERNMENT" FROM INDIVIDUALS IN THE PRIVATE SECTOR PROVIDING GOODS AND SERVICES TO THE WORLD.

Judges, Cops, and Government Employees **RECEIVE**
and Live Off the Taxes Stolen From Others.

They are "Tax RECEIVERS". They just RECEIVE LESS TAXES!

ARTOFLIBERTY.ORG/FACT-CHECK/TAX-RECEIVERS   GOVERNMENT-SCAM.COM

3. Understand That You Are Living off Money Extorted from Your Friends, Family and Neighbors at the Point of a Gun, and While They Are Being Forced to Pay Taxes, You Are NOT Paying Taxes - That, unfortunately, is the "tough love" stone-cold truth of your situation. Taxes are what is extorted from the population to pay your salary. You don't "pay taxes," *you just receive less taxes*. You are *NOT* a tax-payer...
You are a tax-receiver.

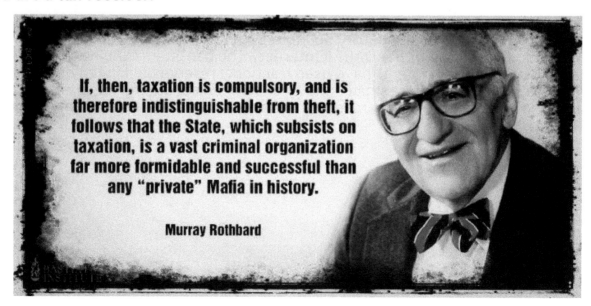

If, then, taxation is compulsory, and is therefore indistinguishable from theft, it follows that the State, which subsists on taxation, is a vast criminal organization far more formidable and successful than any "private" Mafia in history.

Murray Rothbard

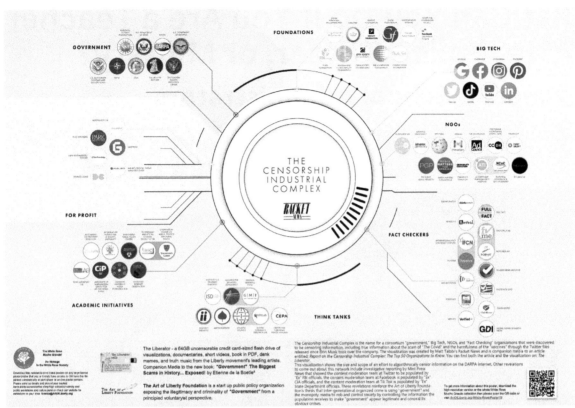

This visualization shows the size and scope of an effort to censor information on the DARPA Internet algorithmically. Other revelations to come out about this network include investigative reporting by Mint Press News that showed <u>the content moderation team at Google is populated by both CIA</u> AND <u>Israeli Mossad/Unit 8200</u>, content moderators at <u>Twitter are populated by "Ex" FBI officials</u>, the content moderation team at <u>Facebook is populated by "Ex" CIA officials.</u> <u>The content moderation team at Tik Tok is inhabited by "Ex" State Department officials.</u> ArtOfLiberty.org/White-Rose

4. Accept my sincerest apologies, and then quit working for organized crime! - *<u>I am genuinely, truly sorry to have to be the one to break this news to you</u>,* especially since I have good friends and family who work in the schools, federal/local government, police, military or are veterans. If you shaved your head and wear/ wore a uniform, if you killed because someone told you to, if you locked up peaceful people for victimless crimes, if you inconvenienced travelers and violated their dignity and privacy if you propagandized and distracted the population from Hollywood, New York, Washington DC, Atlanta, or Langley... it's OK! You are forgiven! We are up against an inter-generational, multi-trillion-dollar propaganda, indoctrination, and control system. I went to government schools and was a Cub Scout and a Boy Scout. It took me a while to overcome the programming. I know it is harder to admit the truth if you are drawing a paycheck. Still, it's time to quit pretending you don't see the government isn't evil, murdering people globally, robbing the population, utterly illegitimate on its face and funded by money stolen from others at the point of a gun. If you are in the system and can't leave...yet... then throw sand in the gears every chance you get: Leak the State's documents, expose the State's crimes, sabotage
the State's ability to track, trace and control peaceful people, and teach the kids in your charge the truth about the system.

What Can You Do If You Are a Teacher, Judge, Police Officer, or Military?

Teachers & School Administrators

Understand the Hidden Curriculum of Mandatory Government Schools: If you still believe you need to work in organized crime's indoctrination centers, then understand the hidden curriculum and help the kids in your charge to understand and question the immorality and illogic of Statism, explain and push back on the obedience techniques being used against them, and help them dodge the debilitation of the vaccines, masks, garbage food, and fluoride in the water fountain.

1. Statism- the indoctrinated belief in the necessity, desirability and legitimacy of government. I.E. How to be a tax slave and submit to organized crime's control system. Understand that this belief system is being slipped to your students as an unethically manipulative pseudo-religion: The "holy documents" of the Con-stitution and completely ignored "Bill of Rights" " the "common prayer" of the pledge of allegiance, and the hymns of the national anthem and Star Spangled Banner, the middle school field trip to "Mecca" (Washington, DC) where the kids are taken to the cathedral of the Capital (which looks like the Vatican for a reason) and to the "temples" of Lincon and Jefferson to see the "deities" where the atmosphere is hushed and reverent, You're an "American".. It's been decided for you!

2. Obedience to authority/government - Subtle unethically manipulative techniques used in the mandatory schools include conditioning kids to governmental "authority" from a young age: can't leave their seat without gov't permission, red, yellow, green troublemaker boards(public shaming), warrantless searches, see-through backpacks, metal detectors, corporal punishment, collective punishment, Pavlovian drill bells, Police officers in schools, scouting and jROTC Uni-forms, repetition, D.A.R.E. program, and the hidden religion of Statism.

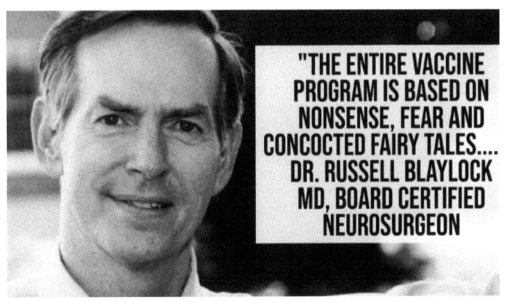

3. Debilitation – Purposely crappy and morality-free education, No focus on the Trivium: Logic, Grammar and Rhetoric. Mandatory mercury and aluminum-laced vaccines, frequently toxic corporate processed foods made with refined grains, refined sugars, Glyphosate and glutamates, rBGH in dairy, and Fluoridated water linked to lower IQ in 50+ studies in the water fountain.

71

Reveal to Your Students What the School System Is Hiding

Libertarianism/Voluntaryism – Not everyone believes in "Government/Gubernare Mente" (Organized Crime), and you don't really owe "Government" or anyone else any money or allegiance because of where you were born. "Government" schools are echo chamber church schools where everyone who has wised up to the scam has been quietly moving their kids to private schools, parochial schools or home-schooling them, leaving only the "true believers."

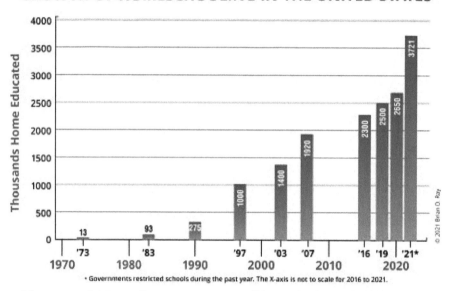

GROWTH OF HOMESCHOOLING IN THE UNITED STATES

More and More Parents Are Pulling Their Kids from the "Free" Government School System

Government Criminality – Whether or not you believe in having a government, the government's mandatory school system and rip-off universities have been hiding/minimizing the government's obvious lies and crimes: From the fraud and inflationary theft of fractional reserve banking to foreign wars based on lies and manufactured intelligence to the CIA's murderous history of Phoenix Program death squads and drug dealing to trillions transferred to private banks and media companies through the TARP/TALF and "Bailouts" to the actuarial impossibility of social security. Be honest with your students about the criminality of the "government."

Begin Organizing for Privatization - Have an open discussion on the need to ultimately privatize operations. Because there can be no legitimate government, there can be no government-funded schools. Teachers and administrators need to begin thinking about how they will privatize school operations and compete for students in a competitive free market. An obvious model would be a transitional year where each school knows it will need to plan for and attract paying students, donations from alumni, and a new business model with teachers getting the freedom to set their own curriculum, rates, co-teaching partnerships, and administrators having to compete for both teachers and students.

Police Officers, DEA, FBI and Other Law Enforcement

I DON'T THINK ALL COPS ARE BAD BECAUSE THE ACTIONS OF A FEW.

I KNOW ALL COPS ARE 'BAD' BECAUSE ALL COPS, AS A CONDITION OF THEIR EMPLOYMENT, SWEAR TO ENFORCE ALL LAWS, INCLUDING LAWS WHICH ARE UNJUST AND INITIATE VIOLENCE ON PEACEFUL PEOPLE. IT'S THE JOB THEY ARE SWORN TO DO. PLEDGING TO SUSPEND MORALITY AND LOGIC IN ORDER TO UNQUESTIONINGLY IMPOSE THE WILL OF PSYCHOPATHS AND SOCIOPATHS ON YOUR FELLOW MAN IS MORALLY UNACCEPTABLE.

SO YES, ALL COPS ARE BAD, BUT NOT BECAUSE OF THE ACTIONS OF A FEW. THERE ARE GOOD PEOPLE, AND THERE ARE COPS WHO ARE OTHERWISE GOOD PEOPLE. BUT THERE ARE NO GOOD COPS.

Police Officers - There is simply no way to sugarcoat this. If you are agreeing to use violence against peaceful people to enforce victimless crimes or raise revenue on your neighbors and community, _**you**_ are the criminal. The uniform and the badge proclaim to the world that you don't understand the basics of morality and are willing to hurt people and extort them for a paycheck.

Here are some options:

1. **Quit and find honorable work.**
2. **Immediately stop the enforcement of victimless crimes, especially lockdowns that allow the organized crime "government" to wage economic warfare on independent businesses.**

3. Go THICKREDLINE and organize your department to say NO! collectively to the enforcement of victimless crimes, lockdowns, mask mandates, red flag laws, and other tyranny. THICKREDLINE is an Art of Liberty Foundation project that we have on the back burner that encourages Sheriffs, Police Chiefs, deputies, and officers to collectively refuse to enforce victimless crimes. This would restore honor to the profession and the deputies and officers themselves.

4. Support organizations like <u>Law Enforcement Action Partnership</u> that organize and educate police, judges and prosecutors on the illegitimacy, counter-productiveness and criminality of victimless crimes.

5. **Begin Positioning Your Sheriff's Office or Police Department for Privatization**
1.   Reduce headcount to only what you need to protect life, liberty and property. You can completely eliminate officers assigned to narcotics, vice, school resource officers, and D.A.R.E programs.
2.   Reduce ridiculous expenditures such as armored vehicles, drones, sting-ray cell phone towers, SWAT Teams and license plate readers.
3.   Refocus the department on preventing real crimes: Murder, Burglaries, Rapes, and Robberies
4.   Become a scholar on police privatization and the existing alternatives from private protection companies like <u>Detroit Threat Management</u> to private communities who are providing their own police services.
5.   Plan for a transition year where tax revenue collected under the threat of force will be replaced with voluntary payments from merchants and private residences. Expect and embrace competition from Brinks, ADT, Westec, and other private security companies.
6.   Create partnerships with alarm system providers, insurance investigators, and other self-interested businesses.
7.   Renounce qualified immunity. Your officers don't get a pass on morality or facing the consequences of their actions.
8.   Think and focus like an entrepreneur on delivering a quality service (crime prevention and restitution vs. retribution) where your officers are focused on protecting the customer vs. raising revenue off the population.

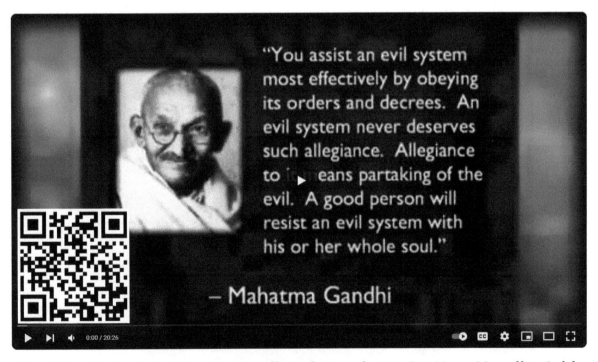

Mark Passio Explains the Immorality of Agreeing to Set Your Morality Aside and Serve as an "Order Follower" in the Police and/or Military
Click on Image or Scan QR Code to Play Video

Judges & Prosectors

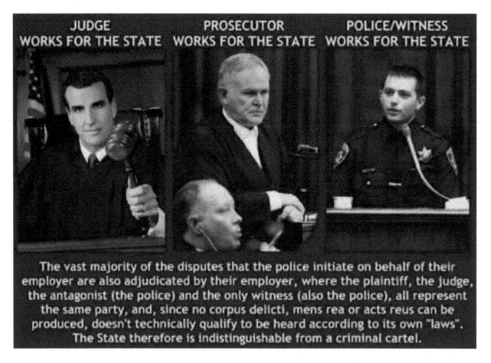

JUDGE WORKS FOR THE STATE | PROSECUTOR WORKS FOR THE STATE | POLICE/WITNESS WORKS FOR THE STATE

The vast majority of the disputes that the police initiate on behalf of their employer are also adjudicated by their employer, where the plaintiff, the judge, the antagonist (the police) and the only witness (also the police), all represent the same party, and, since no corpus delicti, mens rea or acts reus can be produced, doesn't technically qualify to be heard according to its own "laws". The State therefore is indistinguishable from a criminal cartel.

Similar to police officers, if you participate in incarceration or punitive fines for victimless crimes, YOU are the criminal. You are living off money stolen from others at the point of a gun, even if you were "elected" by participants tricked into participating in an immoral and illegitimate system. It would be best if you began organizing your fellow judges on how you will privatize and provide dispute resolution as a service vs. as a monopoly provider kept in business by extortion at the point of a gun.

THERE IS ONLY ONE LAW... DO NO HARM EVERYTHING ELSE IS TYRANNY

Politicians & Elected Officials

privatician noun

pri-vat-ic-ian | \ prī-vət-ti-shən \

Definition of *privatician*

1 : A person running to be an elected official who doesn't believe that "government" is legitimate, desirable or necessary BUT is committed to help their community by serving as an honest steward and community servant, privatizing everything that can be privatized, and focusing on just protecting life, liberty, and property.

2 : Privaticians have taken the Not-A-Politician pledge to never vote for redistribution but to only vote defensively to protect civil and economic liberties.

Be a "Privatician" vs. a Politician - Privaticians are moral and intellectually honest individuals with the courage to admit that "government" is illegitimate, undesirable and unnecessary BUT are willing to serve their communities as honest stewards and community servants by privatizing everything that can be privatized and focusing on protecting life, liberty and property vs. voting for redistribution.

NOT ⬡ POLITICIAN

I am running to be Not-A-<u> NAME OF OFFICE </u>
because I have the integrity to state upfront
that political "authority" is illogical and illegitimate.
It is impossible to acquire "rights" that others
don't have and/or exemptions-from-morality
just because some people choose
to participate in "elections".

I pledge to only use "government" power
defensively to protect life, liberty and property.
I will never vote to rob and redistribute
no matter how worthy the perceived benefits.
I will work to privatize "government" at all levels,
reduce the theft of "taxes", and encourage private
voluntary solutions to societal problems.

I am Not-A-Politician! I am a *Privatician!*

ArtOfLiberty.org/Not-A-Politician

The Military

Tough love for the military: You are not protecting the United States. You are participating in foreign wars and proxy wars being waged by an inter-generational organized crime system tricking you with false flag attacks (9-11) and wars based on lies and manufactured intelligence.

If You Are Stuck in the Military... What to Do About It?

- **Don't kill anyone that isn't actually attacking someone in the United States.** Murder is still murder regardless of what they told you or the costume you wear.
- **Watch the documentary <u>Sir, No Sir!</u>** to understand how GI's in the Vietnam era got organized and stopped that war and then get your buddies organized to say: NO! to murder for hire.
- **Realize you aren't bound by the oath you took due to a well-recognized legal principle called <u>Fraudulent Inducement (Or Fraud in the Inducement)</u>** - because the organized crime "government" lied to you, <u>ran unethically manipulative indoctrination and propaganda on you</u>, and because <u>"government" is illegitimate and immoral on its face</u>, you are not bound by the oath you took because there was "fraud in the inducement"
- **Don't get mad at the messenger...** Get angry with the organized crime system that "ran game on you" with the movies, tell-a-vision shows, social media and video games and tricked you into shaving your head and the uni-form!

Fly Away by Parker Phalen

References and Further Reading from: *The Liberator*
Government-Scam.com/Liberator

9 Reasons to NOT Join the Military by The Wise Sloth
The Military is a Cult - by The Wise Sloth
How and Why Military Basic Training Brain Washes Recruits by The Wise Sloth

Click on the image above or scan the QR Code for a Mark Passio lecture on Cult Indoctrination Techniques Used on the Police and Military

About The Author

EXECUTIVE DIRECTOR

Etienne de la Boetie2 is the founder of the Art of Liberty Foundation, the author of *"Government" – The Biggest Scam in History... Exposed!*, the upcoming book *Voluntaryism - How the Only "ISM" Fair for Everyone Leads to Harmony, Prosperity and Good Karma for All* and the editor of the *Art of Liberty Daily News* on Substack and *Five Meme Friday*, which delivers hard-hitting voluntaryist memes and the best of the alternative media.

He is the author of *The Covid-19 Suspects and Their Ties to Eugenics and Population Control/Reduction* and *Solving Covid - The Covid 19, Eugenics, and Vaccine/Drug Scam Timeline*

The Art of Liberty Foundation

About the Art of Liberty Foundation

A start-up public policy organization: Voluntaryist crime fighters exposing inter-generational organized crime's control of the "government," media and academia. The foundation is the publisher of *"Government" - The Biggest Scam in History... Exposed!- How Inter-Generational Organized Crime Runs the"Government," Media and Academia.*and the upcoming book: *Voluntaryism - How the Only "ISM" Fair for Everyone Leads to Harmony, Prosperity, and Good Karma for All!*

We publish *Important News from the Art of Liberty Foundation* on Substack, which features our original writings and research, *The Daily News*, a free survey of the best of the alternative media, censored videos, and documentaries, and the *Daily News Digest*, a once-per-day-summary of *The Daily News,* and *Five Meme Friday* - a free weekly e-mail or Telegram summary of the best of the alternative media, censored truth videos, and at least five hot, fresh, dank liberty memes every week, and *"Government," Media, and Academia Exposed!* - A Telegram summary of the best mainstream and alternative news stories proving our thesis that all three are being hierarchically controlled by inter-generational organized crime interests.

You can read our 2023 Annual Report here.

Étienne de La Boétie - 1530-1563

The original Etienne de la Boetie was a 16th-century French political philosopher, magistrate, classicist, writer, and poet who was the first to expose the tricks and techniques that rulers use, not just to get obedience, but to get fealty and adoration from their populations. His classic work *The Discourse of Voluntary Servitude* was reproduced and distributed in France to rally the population to resist Nazi occupation and is still read today.

"There are always a few, better endowed than others, who feel the weight of the yoke and cannot restrain themselves from attempting to shake it off: these are the men who never become tamed under subjection. These are in fact the men who, possessed of clear minds and far-sighted spirit, are not satisfied, like the brutish mass, to see only what is at their feet, but rather look about them, behind and before, and even recall the things of the past in order to judge those of the future, and compare both with their present condition. These are the ones who, having good minds of their own, have further trained them by study and learning. Even if liberty had entirely perished from the earth, such men would invent it. For them slavery has no satisfactions, no matter how well disguised."

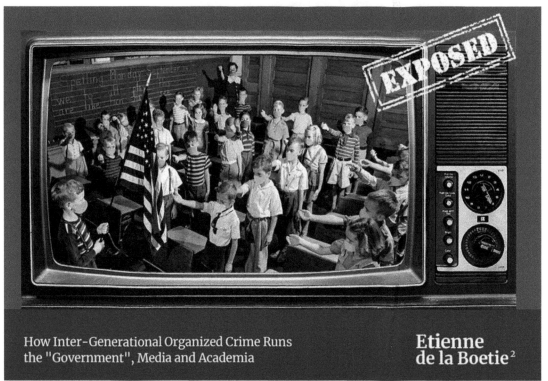

How Inter-Generational Organized Crime Runs
the "Government", Media and Academia

Etienne
de la Boetie²

If you enjoyed this short treatise, then you are going to *love*
"Government" - The Biggest Scam in History... Exposed!
by Etienne de la Boetie2.
Available at Government-Scam.com

The Liberator 64GB

The double-barreled concealed carry of the information war.
Getting Around Internet Censorship
One Flash Drive at a Time.

"Government" - The Biggest Scam in History... Exposed! Is backed up by a credit
card-sized 64GB flash drive of freedom that we call: *The Liberator*. The drive
includes the PDF and ePub versions of *"Government"* plus both uncensorable
evidence of government corruption AND 1000+ dank liberty memes, documentaries,
important books on PDF, short videos, truth music from the liberty movement's
hottest artists, and hundreds of prepping and survivalism resources.
Government-Scam.com/Liberator

Voluntaryism

How the Only "ISM" Fair for Everyone Leads to Harmony, Prosperity and Good Karma for All!

ETIENNE DE LA BOETIE[2]

Please help support our upcoming book _Voluntaryism - How the Only "ISM" Fair for Everyone Leads to Harmony, Prosperity and Good Karma for All!_ This book and _"Government" - The Biggest Scam in History_ expose the problem, Voluntaryism explains the solution and how **_REAL_** Freedom and the free market would lead to a more harmonious and prosperous world.

You can read sample chapters including _What Is Voluntaryism?_, _Assassination Markets to Private Military Defense - Protecting the Country in a Future without "Government,"_ and _Without "Government" What Would We Do About Healthcare?_

You can download two more sample chapters: **What About Physical Protection, Policing and Crime?** and **What About Primary Education?** when you sign up to be notified of the book's release at Voluntaryism-Book.org

Voluntaryism - Why We Don't Need Government!

Help our organization by donating today! Donations go to making a difference for our cause.

$6,637	104	$25,000
Raised	Donations	Goal

$6,637 amount $25,000 amount

Sponsor now →

We are raising **$25,000** to finish up the book, pay for the 1st print run, and a marketing campaign around the book. We have raised **$6,637** from **104** donors and need to raise an additional **$16,363**. You can donate at Voluntaryism-Book.org and we have some great perks to say **_THANK YOU!_**

HOW TO KNOW IF YOU ARE VOLUNTARYIST

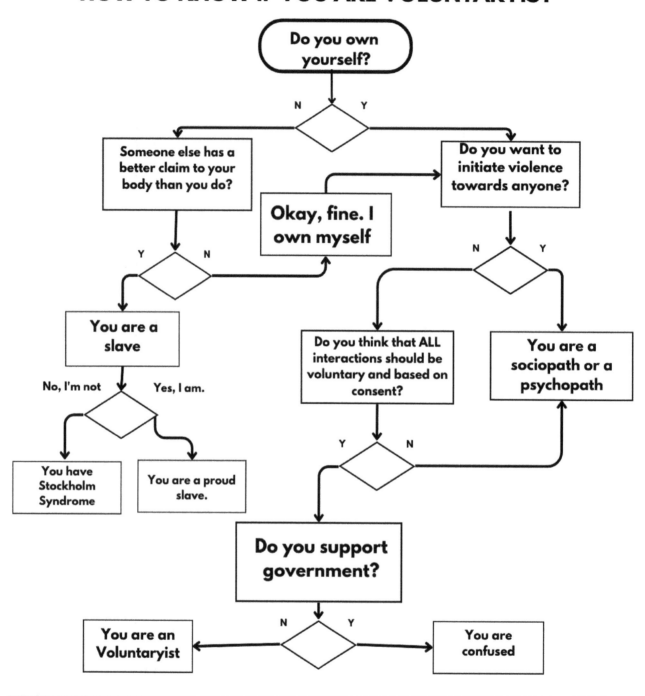

Please Help Support the Art of Liberty Foundation

We have some outstanding premiums to say thank you!

You can donate via Credit Card @ ArtOfLiberty.org/Sponsor, and we have options for offline mail-in donations and cryptocurrency donations below.

Peter S. who upgraded to become a $250 Founding Member on Substack wrote me a wonderful note that I would like to quote from:

"You are doing awesome work, and I am happy to support your efforts. You are helping to launch a totally new way of thinking about governments, for which I am most thankful. I have already bought several copies of your book, with the intention of giving them away to others, something which I have almost never done in my life, since your perspectives and take on history needs desperately to be shared far and wide. Even though as a philosophy major in college--before turning organic farmer—I valued books and ideas very highly, yours is a real paradigm changer!" - Peter S.

Donate Bitcoin Cash:
qqryf3uuua5eh3wr9s7wj6pctppjlm3tm52qmq6749

Donate Bitcoin:
146giKW9aQ13hNeUtE69aSCiKfZSwmzJLL

Donate Monero:
82bhz3dpn9SaJBBXgGRz64TA5DewaK72GKLxXtGF5u
Wz4pGfRWDmKyx6x2c7ZdMhnB6Xz6vXHeCQSNdzmv
2raJJ13jjhHco

Become a Sponsor of the Art of Liberty Foundation
We have some great Perks to say: Thank you!
https://artofliberty.org/sponsorship-program/

www.ingramcontent.com/pod-product-compliance
Ingram Content Group UK Ltd.
Pitfield, Milton Keynes, MK11 3LW, UK
UKHW050853070525
5796UKWH00020B/687